I0505818

Micro and Cottage

Businesses

What You Should Know

And

How to Get Started

Introduction

Very few people are truly happy with their vocation. The average person in the United States goes to a job they hate, in a car they don't own, to pay for things they cannot afford. This is not the way it was supposed to be. I cannot tell you how many people I know that the highlight of their day is a television show or sports event. There is nothing wrong with this, but I believe life is supposed to be so much more.

In this book we are going to go through an evaluation process. Are you the type person who should start your own business? Are you willing to do the research to make an idea come to life? Are you someone who works well on their own, without any supervision? Can you see yourself having more control over your own life? This needs to be a hard and honest look. If you cannot do all of these, a business may not be right for you.

Dedication

I would like to dedicate this book to five people. First I want to dedicate this book to my wife Nicole. For the first time in my life I have truly been blessed with a partner who believes in me. She has stood with me through the good times and the bad and her faith in me has never been shaken. I love you Lubins, you are the greatest.

Second I want to dedicate this book to my parents. They raised me with a strong work ethic, the ability to think outside of the box and the understanding that if I truly put my mind to it I could accomplish anything that I was stubborn enough on which to never give up.

Thirdly I want to dedicate this book to my grandfather Mack Carter. He also instilled in me a strong work ethic, taught me a lot of the things I know about the activities I enjoy most. Above all he taught me the fine art of being a "Make Do" engineer.

Finally, I want to dedicate this book to my Lord and Savior Jesus Christ. I know there are some who think that this part has no reason to be in a book of this type, but I will be honest. Jesus' love for me keeps me going even when I am most wretched. His word the Bible offers both encouragement and correction exactly when I need them most.

TABLE OF CONTENTS

Chapter 1
Why Start a Micro Business?

Almost everything you want to do requires some type of monetary input. If you are working for an hourly wage, you do not have much if any control over how much money you make. I cannot tell you how many times I have heard people try to use a fixed income as a bargaining strategy, but unless someone owns their own business or is paid commission everyone is on a fixed income. At my regular job I am only allowed to get 40 hours a week, that is a fixed income. What I make may not be as tight as others, but it is also not as flexible as some.

What do you need to get out of debt? Build an emergency fund? Do something a little extra around the home? Just become more self reliant? You need to either cut expenses or earn more money. Say you have cut your expenses as far as you can, how can you earn more money if you are paid an hourly wage? Enter the small or micro business. When your sole source of income is a corporation you are at the mercy of someone else who most of the time has never met you. Having a micro or cottage business can give you some security and a sense of fulfillment. So how do you start a micro or cottage business or what business should you start?

It really doesn't matter if your goal for your micro or cottage business is a little extra money or if you want it to become your full-time income, having a source of income that is solely reliant on you is both empowering and a little scary.

Chapter 2
Why You Shouldn't Start Your Own Business?

I can already hear some people saying "What is going on here? I bought this book to help me start a business and this guy very quickly talks about why not to start a business." Stay with me, you will understand.

To Become Rich.

If the only reason you want to start a business is to become rich, don't do it! Stop right now! The truth of the matter is that you probably will not make much of a profit your first year. This is especially true if you have much of a start up cost. Starting small with as little upfront cost as possible is always wise. Your goal should first be to supplement your current income. If you see that this business could become your full-time job, congratulations, that is great.

So You Don't Have To Work As Hard.

Oh, this one is wrong on so many levels. If the business you set up is a "solopreneur", you are marketing, customer service, bookkeeper, chief cook, and bottle washer.

A solopreneur is a person that does all of the workings of a business. They have no employees other than themselves. Many people think solopreneurs are workaholics. Some are, but others just have a drive to accomplish what they have set their mind to do.

As the business owner/operator you have to be there every day. Any problems that arise, you have to take care of them. It may get easier in the long term, but in the beginning you will work your tail off.

You're Looking For An Idea To Make Money Not An Idea You Believe In.

I know for many this one sounds strange too. In the beginning of your business you will almost eat, sleep, and breathe that business. It will most likely be the first thing you think of in the morning and the last thing you think about at night. If you do not believe in what you are doing you will burn out very quickly. Your business should be a passion.

You Do Not Have The Support Of Your Family.

If your family is not onboard or at least supportive of your idea you are probably headed for trouble. Remember I told you that at least in the beginning, the business will be on your mind almost every waking hour? If you do not have the support of your family and if you are all not working to achieve a balance of relationship and work, your relationships will suffer. Notice I did not say it might suffer, I said it will suffer. Do not allow money or your business to become your god or your spouse. A business is not good at being either.

Chapter 3

What is a Small, Micro, and Cottage business?

We are going to focus on micro and cottage businesses, but just for a proper reference I have included the accepted parameters of a small business as well.

Small Business

A small business is actually much larger than I thought, but varies by industry. For the purpose of our discussion a small business is one that has less than 500 employees but more than 5. The business is individually owned (no stockholders). The business was started to make a profit and is not dominant in their field.

Micro Business

A micro business is less than 5 employees normally manned by family and friends usually on a part-time basis. Micro businesses are typically operated out of a home or outbuilding on an individual's property. The average micro business requires no or little start-up capital, usually less than $35,000. Micro businesses can be either service or product based. The average micro business has two employees.

Cottage Business

A Cottage Business is one that is operated from home with typically no more than 2 employees. Cottage businesses tend to be part-time in nature, but do not have to be. The focus is normally on manufacturing or production. Service type businesses are not included in the cottage business model. Knitting, sewing, honey, soaps or other body care products, and things like that tend to dominate. Most things produced in a cottage business tend to be labor intensive.

Chapter 4

The Statistics

According to cfed.org:[1]

4 million micro businesses employ between 1 and 4 people

 over 22 million businesses are operated with no employees beyond the owner

micro businesses generate almost $1 trillion in economic activity annually

74% of micro business owners conduct their business in their local community

52% of all small businesses are home-based.

That is power, and it is growing.

---

[1] http://cfed.org/assets/pdfs/FactFile_May2013.pdf

Chapter 5

Personal inventory

Now that we have a good understanding of the types of smaller businesses, we will dive into what you will need to look at to decide what business you should build for ourselves. We have to take an honest look at ourselves to decide what business we might do well in.

What Are Your Skills And Talents?

In order to make anything a profitable business, you must lean on your strengths. If you are really good at knitting, cooking, or sewing these may be things you could look at offering as a business. Homemade items tend to bring a premium from those who care about such things, but the items have to be quality. If you are good at teaching, you might find that teaching others the skills that you are good at may make you more money than making things and selling them.

What Do You Enjoy?

It doesn't really matter how good you are at something, if you don't enjoy it, you will not stick with it. As an example I do not like mowing the yard. Mowing the yard is my idea of absolutely nothing left to do. There are some people who truly enjoy mowing the yard. Now I love being outside and doing a variety of things, but riding back and forth just watching grass fly is not fun for me. If I were going to start a new business, I would not start a lawn care business. I might start a landscaping business and subcontract out the mowing part, but I do not want to have to spend several days a week mowing.

What tools do you have now?

If you are wanting to start a business and not go into any debt in the process, you will have to use what you have on hand now. If you are really good at construction or repair and you have some basic tools, this is something that you could start anytime you wanted. If you are thinking about going into lawn care and you only have a push mower, you could start your business, but the operations of the business would be greatly restricted by your equipment. The equipment you have will help you determine either what business you wish to start or how soon you could start your business.

Chapter 6

Taxes

There are tax benefits for owning a micro or cottage business, but there are also tax pitfalls.

Tax Benefits

Things that are 100% tax deductible:

- Tools that are purchased exclusively for use in the business.
- All marketing costs i.e. business cards, newspaper ads, phonebook ads, radio spots etcetera.
- All business related travel.
- All business related education.
- All true business dinners. (Some people go crazy on this one and get themselves into trouble)
- Business Insurance. (liability and possible bonding)

There are other things that are partially tax deductible. If you have a home office, you can take a home office deduction. If you use your personal vehicle for business use the business related mileage is also tax deductible.

Taxes can get complicated in a hurry. All of your business related income expenses have to be entered on their own form called a schedule C. Please be aware that the Internal Revenue Service (IRS) will consider you self employed. A self employed person must pay self employment taxes. That is 12.6% of your income; this is your Social Security tax, plus you have to pay a 2.9% Medicare tax. Yup, you have to pay 15.4% in taxes before you even get to income taxes.

Social Security, Medicare, and Employment Insurance taxes must be paid on every employee. There are some exemptions for family members.

If you are selling a product you will have to collect sales taxes. Oh and don't forget the Affordable Care Act. Small businesses have an exemption from the Affordable Care Act till they reach 50 employees. Most of the ideas we will talk about here wouldn't reach that threshold.

The taxes involved with a micro business can quickly become at least a headache and at most a nightmare. Please, talk to a tax professional about all of this, but taxes should not be a deciding factor in whether or not to start a small business.

Chapter 7

Local Laws

Okay, this one is a biggie. You will have to talk to someone at your local courthouse to determine what laws will apply to your new business idea. There are some cities that are very anti small/micro business. There have been cities that have shut down bake sales for local nonprofit organizations because they did not purchase the proper permits. Police have shut down children's lemonade stands. Officials have confiscated and/or destroyed garden produce because licenses were not in order all under the guise of trying to make sure people are safe.

Common Law Issues

If you are a good cook and enjoy doing so, you might want to start a business where you cook for those who are physically impaired. You may find that it is illegal for you to cook meals in your home and take them to your customers, but perfectly legal for them to hire you to cook those meals in their home.

In certain cities and communities you may learn that in order to be paid to cut someone's grass you have to attend a class and be certified as a lawn care technician. There is a community not far from where I live in which that is the case, oh and the class is $300.00 a year. If you just want to make a little side money that alone could knock that idea out. Ask questions, learn as much as you can or you could face fines. You may learn that you live in an area where everything is regulated. I hope not, but it does happen.

Business License

In some smaller cities and towns obtaining a business license is no big deal. You simply go to the county courthouse or city hall and pay a tax to be able to operate a business in their area. Other cities are not so easy. While I was operating a carriage service (you will find out more about that later). I was contacted about providing my service for a wedding in Huntsville, Alabama. I wanted to do everything right. So I called city hall and asked what I needed to do to get a business license. As soon as I explained what my business was they informed me that I would have to come to the city commissioners meeting and be willing to answer questions and that they would vote on whether or not I would be granted a business license.

It turned out not being a big deal. I did have to wait for 2 hours before my petition came up and there were several questions, but I had photos and I had copies of other cities' business licenses that I had. After all of that I was granted the "privilege" of buying a business license in their town by a 4 to 1 vote. Yup, someone voted against allowing me to drive my carriage in their town.

Chapter 8

Location, Location, Location

This is just a fact of life. Where you live determines some of the types of businesses that you can start. The higher the population density and socioeconomic scale your area is, the easier it will be to start a micro or cottage business. I am not saying that if you are very rural you cannot start a business. What I am saying is the more rural you are might determine some businesses unfeasible and will mean that you may have to work harder to create a market or that you will have to deal with distribution on a larger scale that someone who is suburban or urban.

Pet sitting or babysitting businesses tend to do well in suburban environments. If you were to try to start a pet sitting business in a very rural area, it could quickly turn into a temporary farm hand business. Nothing wrong with doing temporary farm hand work if that is what you like, but the business will change based on where you are.

Chapter 9
Marketing

I know it may seem a little strange that I am covering marketing before we talk about business ideas, but how you intend to market your idea will have a direct impact on how your business will grow and what will become the public's perception of you and your company. Some types of marketing will work great for some businesses and do little to nothing for others. Let's look at a few marketing methods.

Flyers

Flyers can be an effective low cost marketing method. You are in control of the appearance of the flyer. There are sites online that will let you create and print flyers. Think about the information you want to share and the image you want to create.

Pull tab flyers are great. They have all of the information that you want on them and potential clients have the ability to tear off a small tab and have your contact information handy. Flyers should be checked on regularly. If you have a flyer up at say a local grocery store, having a few tabs missing will actually encourage someone to take a tab as well. If all of the tabs are gone or if the flyers look bad it looks like you do not care about your business.

Business Cards

Every business should have business cards. They can be simple. You can design your business cards yourself and print them on good card stock or you can use a printing company. Vista print (vistaprint.com) allows you to design cards and have them printed affordably.

Your business card design should be clean and informative. A card that is too busy is not appealing at all. Again, think about the image you are trying to convey.

Social Media

Even with all of the changes, social media is still the best way to get the word out about a new business for free. You can create a business page and invite your friends and family to like the page. Post information about your services or products. Use lots of pictures. If for example you are starting a pet sitting business, have pictures of you playing with someone's pet.

Facebook allows you to promote a page. When promoting you can select a geographic area where you want the page to be promoted or boosted. For businesses that are just getting started this is not a bad idea, but I would use all of the free and less expensive options first. Definitely set up a business page that is free.

Newspaper Ads

Newspaper ads can be both good and bad. If you don't know anyone that reads your local paper, that means very few people do. I have made the mistake of placing an ad in a local paper and not have a single person call to inquire about my service. Newspaper ads can be expensive as well. Do your research. The newspaper should be able to give you information on distribution and readership.

If your community has a paper that is delivered free to households in your area look at that one first. A county a little north of me has what is called a shopper's guide. It is delivered to every household in the county on Wednesdays. Word ads in this paper are not very expensive. I tried an experiment. One week I placed a word ad three times in the same issue, the next week I placed a display ad. I received three times more calls from the word ads as I did with the display ad and the word ads were half the cost.

Word of Mouth

Word of mouth has always been the best form of marketing and I believe always will be. If people are saying good things about your business you will get more clients. How do you get people talking about your business? That varies by type of business, but I will cover selling eggs.

When I was selling eggs as a source of extra income, I started with my neighbors. I went to their house and gave them a dozen eggs. Yup, I gave them the eggs. I told them that if they liked them they could purchase more in the future and I told them how much I wanted per dozen. About 1/3 of the people I gave eggs to became regular customers. They told their friends and the business grew to the point where I had a waiting list of people who wanted my chickens eggs.

There you go. That should be more than enough information to help you decide what type of marketing you will want to use for your micro or cottage business.

Chapter 10

Low or No Cost Business Ideas

We are going to talk about as many low or no cost business ideas as I can come up with. For the purpose of this discussion a low start up cost business is one that can be started for less than $500. This price will include all initial capital equipment, advertising, and if necessary licenses. Since I am including licenses this list will vary greatly based on your local government's greed.

Pet Sitting

Pet sitting can be a great micro business. Pet sitting tends to have the least regulations and can be advertised with word of mouth fairly easily. Initial start up cost very small if any. Of course you have to like animals and you have to be willing to welcome small pets into your home.

There are two ways to set up a pet sitting business. Way number one is to have the owners bring the pet to your home and you take care of them there. Way number two is to take care of the pets in their own home. The first way is easier and has a lower initial cost. The second way allows you to provide value added services that can dramatically increase your income.

Things to consider:

- **Get to know the animal.** The last thing you want is to agree to keep a dog or cat in your home only to find out that the animal is not friendly or even worse the animal is a biter. Being bitten by a small dog hurts. It hurts badly. If you have children you will need to know if the animal likes children.
- **The animal's veterinary information.** If something were to happen you will need to know where to take the animal.
- **If the animal has to go to the vet who will pay?** It is really bad to get paid $25.00 a day (or whatever) only to have the animal get sick and you wind up owing hundreds of dollars of veterinary expenses.
- **The animal's health history.** If a pet requires medicine or has allergies, you need to know.

- **Contracts.** Sorry but if you are going to do much pet sitting you will need a good contract. This will detail how long the pet will be with you, the payment terms, what to do in case the pet needs medical attention, what you will do with the pet if it is abandoned, and a lot more. You can have an attorney draw up a contract for you or you can create your own at http://www.free-legal-document.com/pet-sitting-contract.html. If you only pet sit for family and friends you may not need this, but trust me. I have had a pet left with me and had to find it another home.
- **Liability insurance.** If you are going to take care of the animal in their owner's home, liability insurance is a must. Even if everything goes great, if you break something in your client's home you are in for problems. However; if you have liability insurance you can inform your client and file the incident on your liability insurance.
- **Do a little extra.** If you really want to make a name for yourself pet sitting, do something a little extra. It could be something as simple as brushing out the pet or even bathing the pet. Taking the

extra step will really get your customers talking.

Baby Sitting

What was once only thought of as a part-time job for teenage girls has turned into a business in many areas of the country. Like pet sitting word of mouth is your best advertisement and there is very little start-up costs. Things that need to be considered are: Will you be keeping the children in your home or the home of the parents? How late will the parents be out? What do they expect you to do while you are taking care of their children? You must have contact information and know any allergies the children have. Being certified in CPR is a big plus.

Like pet sitting, do a little extra. If keeping the children in their home this could be washing the dishes after you have fed the children or just cleaning up the living room a little. This will leave a lasting impact.

House Cleaning

You will need a fairly affluent market in order for this to be feasible. As people's schedules continue to fill with all kinds of things many are finding less and less times to do things at home. I have known several people who hired individuals to clean their homes. This does not require much to get started, just an attention to detail and a little bit of OCD. Most times you will be using supplies that are provided by the homeowner. The only extra things you will need are the specialty cleaning items that you must have.

Garden or Farm Produce

I have never produced so many chicken eggs that I couldn't sell them all, but I have produced so much squash that I couldn't give it away. With farm produce you have to be smart. If everyone with a garden produces something in your area, you are not going to make a lot of money producing that item. Squash and zucchini are good examples, not everyone likes them and those that do can grow them fairly easily. These produce in such abundance that if you have three plants you will be trying to get rid of squash and zucchini.

Any business that deals with animals can do well as a small business. Eggs, at least around here, are a very easy sell. Raising chickens for meat has also done really well locally. Selling hogs, beef cattle, raw milk, quail, you name it, can do really well. There can be a start-up cost but it doesn't have to be high. If you have the room this can be an idea for you. Remember to check local laws. Here in Alabama if you sell raw milk it must be labeled Not For Human Consumption.

Economies of Scale. With many businesses you will run into something called economies of scale. What economies of scale means is that as you produce more of an item or type of item, the cost of production for each additional item goes down. Why is this the case? Once you have your capital investments done you do not have to do that again. Your fixed costs are set.

Handyman

If you are a decent carpenter or good at repairs you probably already have your tools. This type of small business can be as big or as small as you like. In many areas basic repairs are not regulated. If you can do basic plumbing and/or basic electrical you could be in good. Plumbing and electrical tend to be more regulated than basic carpentry.

Teaching

If you excel at a skill that others would like to learn, teaching can be an awesome side business. Crafting makes for easily started classes. Knitting, sewing, cooking, and several more do well. I have taught several classes over the years. I have taught basic dog obedience, tracking, competition obedience, foraging, and am now teaching basic preparedness courses. Teach something you are passionate about.

Lawn Service

A lawn service was the first business I ever owned, though I didn't see it that way at the time. When I started I actually used a push mower and a rake. Most times I pushed the mower from yard to yard. My dad bought a riding mower and I was in heaven. I drove the mower from place to place. It was not a big or even a very professional business. I was just a young teen trying to earn money to buy the things I wanted, but it was a start.

Homemade Items

I am continually astounded by the growing interest in homemade beauty care and homemade cleaning products. I know several people who are making a nice side income making lip balms and beauty care products. This is something that my wife and I are going to do this summer. Not to sell, we just want to move away from all of the chemicals.

Chapter 11

Medium Level Initial Investment

All of these can still be a micro business, but can be scaled up or down dependent on the demand. For us medium level initial investment means over $500. These can still be a small family operation.

Welding

If you have the skill, this is a great business, especially if you have a mobile welding unit. Welding is a skill that if you do well you can be in high demand. I have personally paid someone to weld for me because I did not have the equipment.

Scrap Metal

The reason I included this business idea here instead of low or no cost ideas is because you will need a pickup truck and possibly a trailer.

There are people who make decent money driving around the community looking for old appliances or even wrecked cars that have been placed on back lots. In our local paper there are ads weekly for free pickup of any and all scrap metal. I have sold scrap metal in the past and if you keep an eye on the recycle prices this type of business can be profitable.

Pallet Reconstruction

Depending on where you live this one could be easy or tough to get into. Retail and manufacturing businesses get most of their supplies and stock on pallets. Many of these pallets are broken. You may be able to get these broken pallets for free. Once you have these pallets you rebuild them and sell them to other companies that need them, sometimes to the very companies that you got them from. I know of 5 businesses within 30 miles that do this, the smallest of which employs 10 people. You could do this by yourself. Equipment you would need to make this profitable would include a pickup truck and trailer, an air compressor and nail gun, and a lot of muscle. You will be salvaging good parts from some to make complete pallets of others.

Elite Services

In the past I have owned and operated two businesses that could be called elite services. What do I mean by elite services? Services that are only used on special occasions and would be considered a luxury. A limousine service would fall into this category but would have a very high initial investment.

Dove Releases. You may have seen one of these. They normally occur at either weddings or funerals. White "doves" are released either from a cage or a basket. They fly around, look real pretty and then go home. Here is a little secret. The white doves that are released at these ceremonies are actually white homing pigeons. Pigeons breed like rats so it is easy to expand your release business. I started out with 3 pairs and by the time I sold the birds I had 20 and some of the birds that were released didn't make it home. Make sure that you purchase birds that are less than 6 months old. If you purchase birds much older than that, as soon as you let them out of their loft they will go to their previous home and the owner can keep them or sell them again. Sorry I don't have any photos of my old business, but I can tell you I have been out of this business for about 12 years and I got a call the other day asking if I still did releases.

You can learn more about purchasing white homing pigeons at The American White Dove Release Association. I used the old Department of War training guide you can find that at the following address:

http://www.history.navy.mil/research/library/online-reading-room/title-list-alphabetically/i/homing-pigeons.html.

Oh, by the way. Do not do a release on opening day of dove season. Very few will make it home. Trust me I know.

Carriage Service. This one can be a fairly large initial investment, but if you hustle you can make some good money. I purchased my carriages from Robert's Carriages in Canada. At the time they were very affordable and delivered right to my farm. I charged $300 for two hours for a wedding and did things like proms, festivals and parades. Not only did this provide me a good income while I was going to school, I was able to sell the business when I was ready to get out of the business. I was able to find some old photos of the carriage service.

Here are my words of warning on a carriage service.

- Have a good contract. I have had to stand in the rain for hours waiting on a wedding to end, that by the way ended late, very late. Oh and I got a $1.00 tip
- Presentation is everything. If you are not good at decorating, learn. Some wedding parties will want to decorate themselves, have something in the contract about additional non riding hours.
- Have a cancellation policy.
- Require a deposit
- Decide where you will offer your services. When I was running the carriage service, I covered all of North Alabama. At one time I had to have business licenses in 6 cities all in the same year. Research is key.

Chapter 12

Final Thoughts

Is this a complete list? Oh no. This list could go on forever. Figure out what people want or need and be able to give it to them. Your creativity and drive will help ensure your success. If you run into roadblocks it does not mean your business is a bad idea.

Proverbs 16:3 Commit your work to the Lord, and your plans will be established.

Do your math well. The last thing you want to do is price your goods or services too high or too low. Both will run you out of business. One will destroy your business by wearing you out and the other by rusting you out. Either way you are still out.

Don't be afraid to reach out to others who are doing the same thing in different areas. Thanks to the internet we have networking abilities that have never been seen before. There is always someone who will be willing to answer your question.

I hope this book has inspired you to at least look into starting your own business and taking a little more control over your future and your self reliance. Being your own boss at least part of the time is one more way we can all....

Bring Rural Back

About The Author

Gregg is a writer, blogger, homesteader, preparedness teacher and make do engineer. He lives with his wife and children in North Central Alabama.

He has a bachelor's degree in Business Management with a minor in Entrepreneurship from Athens State University and graduated with honors.

He has owned and operated five businesses. Two he sold, one was destroyed by the April 2011 tornados, and two he is still working today.

You can follow along with Gregg as he continues on his journey to greater self reliance on his blog www.theruraleconomist.com

www.ingramcontent.com/pod-product-compliance
Lightning Source LLC
Chambersburg PA
CBHW070923180526
45168CB00005B/2127